D0386258

VALENTINE'S DAY

By EMMA CARLSON BERNE

Illustrations by AARON CUSHLEY

Music by MARK OBLINGER

IOWA CITY
DISCARD
from Iowa City Public Library
JAN 2018
PUBLIC LIBRARY

CANTATA
LEARNING

WWW.CANTATALEARNING.COM

Published by Cantata Learning
1710 Roe Crest Drive
North Mankato, MN 56003
www.cantatalearning.com

Copyright © 2018 Cantata Learning

C A N T A T A
L E A R N I N G

All rights reserved. No part of this publication may be reproduced in any form without written permission from the publisher.

Library of Congress Cataloging-in-Publication Data
Names: Berne, Emma Carlson, author. | Cushley, Aaron illustrator. | Oblinger, Mark, composer.
Title: Valentine's Day / by Emma Carlson Berne ; illustrations by Aaron Cushley ; music by Mark Oblinger.
Description: North Mankato, Minnesota : Cantata Learning, [2018] | Series: Holidays in rhythm and rhyme | Audience: Ages 5–7. | Audience: Grades: K to Grade 3.
Identifiers: LCCN 2017028197 (print) | LCCN 2017047967 (ebook) | ISBN 9781684101757 (ebook) | ISBN 9781684101245 (hardcover : alk. paper) | ISBN 9781684101948 (paperback : alk. paper)
Subjects: LCSH: Valentine's Day—Juvenile literature. | Valentine's Day—Juvenile poetry.
Classification: LCC GT4925 (ebook) | LCC GT4925 .B47 2018 (print) | DDC 394.2618—dc23
LC record available at https://lccn.loc.gov/2017028197

Book design and art direction, Tim Palin Creative
Editorial direction, Kellie M. Hultgren
Music direction, Elizabeth Draper
Music arranged and produced by Mark Oblinger

Printed in the United States of America in North Mankato, Minnesota.
122017
0378CGS18

ACCESS THE MUSIC!

SCAN CODE WITH MOBILE APP

CANTATALEARNING.COM

TIPS TO SUPPORT LITERACY AT HOME

WHY READING AND SINGING WITH YOUR CHILD IS SO IMPORTANT

Daily reading with your child leads to increased academic achievement. Music and songs, specifically rhyming songs, are a fun and easy way to build early literacy and language development. Music skills correlate significantly with both phonological awareness and reading development. Singing helps build vocabulary and speech development. And reading and appreciating music together is a wonderful way to strengthen your relationship.

READ AND SING EVERY DAY!

TIPS FOR USING CANTATA LEARNING BOOKS AND SONGS DURING YOUR DAILY STORY TIME

1. As you sing and read, point out the different words on the page that rhyme. Suggest other words that rhyme.

2. Memorize simple rhymes such as Itsy Bitsy Spider and sing them together. This encourages comprehension skills and early literacy skills.

3. Use the questions in the back of each book to guide your singing and storytelling.

4. Read the included sheet music with your child while you listen to the song. How do the music notes correlate to the words of the song?

5. Sing along on the go and at home. Access music by scanning the QR code on each Cantata book, or by using the included CD. You can also stream or download the music for free to your computer, smartphone, or mobile device.

Devoting time to daily reading shows that you are available for your child. Together, you are building language, literacy, and listening skills.

Have fun reading and singing!

Valentine's Day is all about love! In ancient times, some **saints** were named Valentine. People had special days to remember these saints. Later, Valentine's Day turned into a day to **celebrate** love and **friendship**. Each year, on February 14th, we give our family and friends cards and drawings. Sometimes we give candy or little presents. Most of all, we tell them how much we love them.

Let's sing about Valentine's Day together!

HAPPY
LOVE
DAY

On the fourteenth of February,

when winter skies are gray,

I cut out hearts, pink and red,

making cards for Valentine's Day.

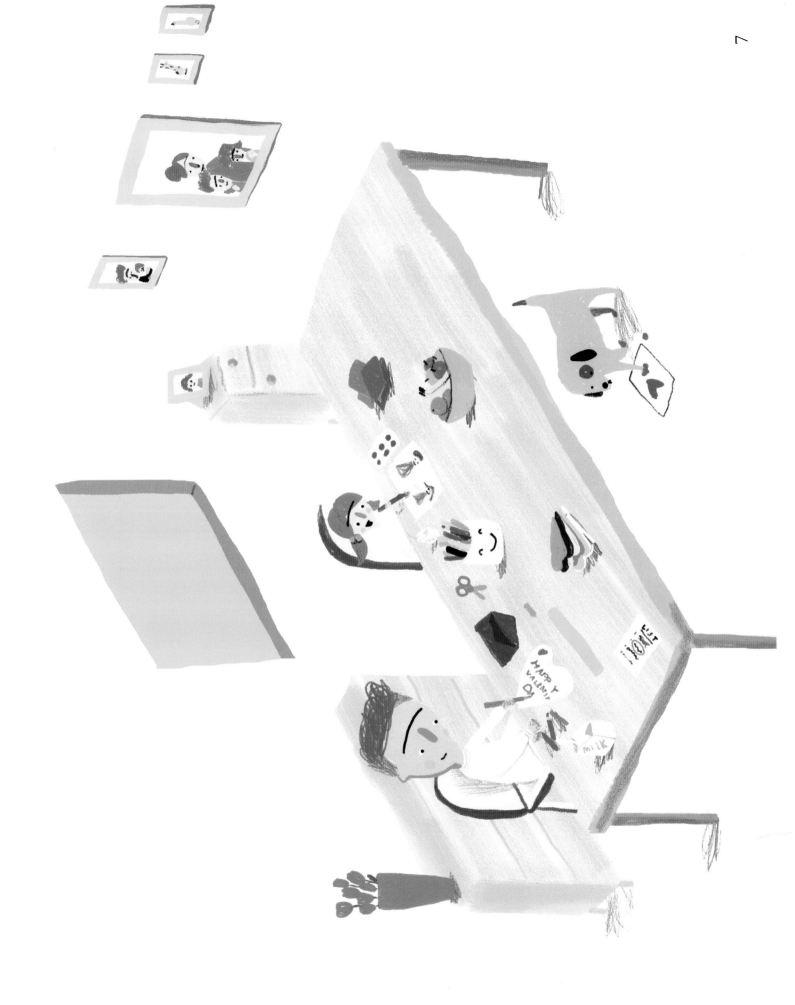

Wintertime we wish away,
but we have love on Valentine's Day.

Hearts of pink and red we share
to show the world that we care.

Now I'm in the kitchen.

I'm baking valentine treats.

I roll the **dough** and stamp out hearts.

I'll give my friends these sweets!

Wintertime we wish away,
but we have love on Valentine's Day.

Hearts of pink and red we share
to show the world that we care.

The school day is almost over.

Let's pass out candy hearts!

I give away my valentines.

That's my favorite part!

Wintertime we wish away,
but we have love on Valentine's Day.

Hearts of pink and red we share
to show the world that we care.

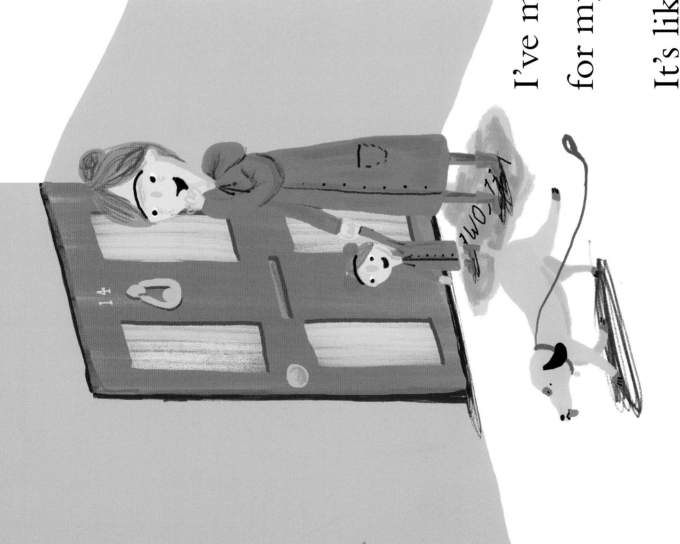

I've made a secret valentine for my whole family, too.

It's like a hug on paper saying, "I love you!"

Wintertime we wish away,
but we have love on Valentine's Day.

Hearts of pink and red we share
to show the world that we care.

SONG LYRICS
Valentine's Day

On the fourteenth of February,
when winter skies are gray,
I cut out hearts, pink and red,
making cards for Valentine's Day.

Wintertime we wish away,
but we have love on Valentine's Day.
Hearts of pink and red we share
to show the world that we care.

Now I'm in the kitchen.
I'm baking valentine treats.
I roll the dough and stamp out hearts.
I'll give my friends these sweets!

Wintertime we wish away,
but we have love on Valentine's Day.
Hearts of pink and red we share
to show the world that we care.

The school day is almost over.
Let's pass out candy hearts!
I give away my valentines.
That's my favorite part!

Wintertime we wish away,
but we have love on Valentine's Day.
Hearts of pink and red we share
to show the world that we care.

I've made a secret valentine
for my whole family, too.
It's like a hug on paper
saying, "I love you!"

Wintertime we wish away,
but we have love on Valentine's Day.
Hearts of pink and red we share
to show the world that we care.

Valentine's Day

Pop/Doo Wop
Mark Oblinger

Verse

A   F#min   D   E   F#min   A/E

1. On the four - teenth of Feb - ru - ar - y, when win - ter skies are gray, I cut out hearts,

D   A   D   E   A   F#min   A/E   D   A   D   E   A

pink and red, mak - ing cards for Val - en - tine's Day.

Chorus A   F#min   D   E   A

Win - ter - time, we wish a - way, but we have love on Val - en - tine's Day.

F#min   A/E   D   A   D   E   A

Hearts of pink and

F#min   D   E   A

red we share to show the world that we care.

Verse 2
Now I'm in the kitchen.
I'm baking valentine treats.
I roll the dough and stamp out hearts.
I'll give my friends these sweets!

Chorus

Verse 3
The school day is almost over.
Let's pass out candy hearts!
I give away my valentines.
That's my favorite part!

Chorus

Verse 4
I've made a secret valentine
for my whole family, too.
It's like a hug on paper
saying, "I love you!"

Chorus

ACCESS THE MUSIC!

SCAN CODE WITH MOBILE APP

CANTALEARNING.COM

GLOSSARY

celebrate—to do activities to mark a special, happy time

dough—a mixture of flour and water, sometimes milk and eggs, for baking

friendship—when two people care about each other and spend time together

saints—special religious people who are remembered after their deaths

---

TO LEARN MORE

Mathiowetz, Claire. *Valentine's Day Crafts*. North Mankato, MN: Child's World, 2017.

Pettiford, Rebecca. *Valentine's Day*. Minneapolis: Jump!, 2016.

Sebra, Richard. *It's Valentine's Day!* Minneapolis: Lerner, 2017.

GUIDED READING ACTIVITIES

1. Having parties, baking cookies, and making valentines are some of the Valentine's Day activities this book talks about. What are your favorite ways to celebrate Valentine's Day?

2. Valentine's Day is all about love and caring. What is one way you show your family you care about them? What is one way you show your friends you care?

3. Some people are lonely on Valentine's Day. Can you think of a person you know who might not get lots of valentines? Why do you think he or she might like one?